For the Teacher

This reproducible study guide to use in conjunction with a specific novel consists of lessons for guided reading. Written in chapter-by-chapter format, the guide contains a synopsis, pre-reading activities, vocabulary and comprehension exercises, as well as extension activities to be used as follow-up to the novel.

In a homogeneous classroom, whole class instruction with one title is appropriate. In a heterogeneous classroom, reading groups should be formed: each group works on a different novel on its reading level. Depending upon the length of time devoted to reading in the classroom, each novel, with its guide and accompanying lessons, may be completed in three to six weeks.

Begin using NOVEL-TIES for reading development by distributing the novel and a folder to each child. Distribute duplicated pages of the study guide for students to place in their folders. After examining the cover and glancing through the book, students can participate in several pre-reading activities. Vocabulary questions should be considered prior to reading a chapter; all other work should be done after the chapter has been read. Comprehension questions can be answered orally or in writing. The classroom teacher should determine the amount of work to be assigned, always keeping in mind that readers must be nurtured and that the ultimate goal is encouraging students' love of reading.

The benefits of using NOVEL-TIES are numerous. Students read good literature in the original, rather than in abridged or edited form. The good reading habits, formed by practice in focusing on interpretive comprehension and literary techniques, will be transferred to the books students read independently. Passive readers become active, avid readers.

Novel-Ties® are printed on recycled paper.

SYNOPSIS

Six-year-old Ramona Quimby usually needed her older sister Beatrice to be her champion. That was true until the day Ramona came to her sister's defense when the sixth-grade boys teased her about her nickname, Beezus. Instead of being grateful, Beezus simply felt embarrassed by her little sister.

As the story begins, it is well into summer. Ramona is bored and eager to start first grade. She also looks forward to the construction of an additional room to their family's house so that she will no longer have to share a room with Beezus.

Unfortunately, reality does not measure up to Ramona's dreams about first grade. She feels misunderstood by her teacher, Mrs. Griggs, who does not appreciate Ramona's show-and-tell account of the home renovation. In contrast, her sister Beezus is very happy with her new class and her teacher, Mr. Cardoza.

As the days pass, Ramona continues to be at odds with Mrs. Griggs and with her classmates. In anticipation of Parents' Night, Mrs. Griggs asks the class to make "wise owls." Susan copies from Ramona and gets complimented on her excellent drawing. Torn between being called a copycat or a tattletale, Ramona feels over-whelmed and destroys Susan's owl. Although she receives some sympathy at home, her parents insist that she apologize to Susan. Ramona feels humiliated. To make matters worse, the new bedroom presents problems. Ramona has nightmares sleeping there alone, away from the center of the house. Frustrations accumulate when Ramona's progress report indicates that her school work is satisfactory, but she needs to practice greater self-control.

Finally, Dad comes to the rescue. Calling Ramona his spunky girl, he is able to lighten her spirits, encouraging her to fight her fears and disappointments. She gets a chance to show her bravery when she defends herself against a large dog. When this story is told at school, Ramona finally receives the recognition she needs.

PRE-READING ACTIVITIES

1. Have you read any other "Ramona" book? What do you remember about Ramona, her older sister Beezus, and their parents? How do the sisters get along with each other? Do you remember a funny incident from one of the other books? Describe it.

2. Read each of these phrases. Write a "B" in front of an action that is brave. Write a "C" in front of an action that is cowardly. Write "B-C" if the action could be both.

    1. _____ admitting that you did something wrong

    2. _____ walking away from a group of children who tease you

    3. _____ protecting your friend in a fight with a bully

    4. _____ protecting a young child from an oncoming car

    5. _____ telling the teacher when someone has copied your work

    6. _____ telling an adult about something that scares you

    7. _____ staying out of school because you forgot to do your homework

    8. _____ practicing riding your bike when you keep falling off

    9. _____ running away from something that looks like a ghost

    10. _____ saying you feel sick the day of a test

3. What is your position in your family? Are you oldest, youngest, middle, or an only child?

    _____

    What two things do you like best about your position?

    _____

    What two things do you dislike about your position?

    _____

    If you had your choice, what would be your position in your family? Tell why you feel as you do.

    _____

    _____

CHAPTER 1

Vocabulary: Draw a line from each word on the left to its meaning on the right. Then use the numbered words to fill in the blanks in the sentences below.

1. errands   a. trust in oneself
2. triumphant   b. quiet; controlled
3. reluctant   c. extremely annoying
4. subdued   d. victorious; successful
5. confidence   e. short journeys for specific purposes
6. exasperating   f. unwilling

. . . .

1. It was _____ to have to tell my little sister over and over again that she must not touch my clothes.

2. My friends understood that I had to complete my _____ before I could meet them at the playground.

3. When you are in the library, please speak in a(n) _____ voice.

4. Wondering whether the traffic would stop, I was _____ to cross the street.

5. A(n) _____ smile crossed her face when she realized she was first across the finish line.

6. My _____ was shattered when I knew that I would not finish my project in time as I had promised.

> Read to find out how Ramona comes to her big sister's defense.

Questions:

1. Why was Ramona eager to tell her mother what had happened in the park?

2. How did Ramona feel about what had happened? Why?

Chapter 1 (cont.)

3. What did Mrs. Quimby tell Beezus to do if she were teased again?

4. How did Ramona feel about her summer vacation? Why did she feel this way?

5. How did Beezus get her nickname?

Questions for Discussion:

1. Why do you think Mrs. Quimby seemed amused by Ramona's story?

2. Do you think it is wise to ignore people who tease or bully you? Is there any other strategy you might use?

Sequence: Number these events in the order in which they occurred.

_____ Ramona is proud of defending Beezus.

_____ The boys laugh at Ramona's sermon.

_____ Some boys tease Beezus.

_____ Beezus is embarrassed.

_____ Ramona comes to her sister's defense.

_____ Ramona tells her mother what happened.

Writing Activity:

Write about a time when you were teased. Tell whether someone came to your rescue or whether you had to defend yourself. Indicate whether you enjoyed the teasing and if it continued after the first event.

CHAPTER 2: MRS. QUIMBY'S SECRET

Vocabulary: Synonyms are words with similar meanings. Draw a line from each word in column A to its synonym in column B. Then use the words in column A to fill in the blanks in the sentences below.

A	B
1. jaunty	a. excitement
2. public	b. open
3. indignant	c. lively
4. virtuous	d. angry
5. enthusiasm	e. moral

. . . .

1. The audience's _____ for the play was shown by their long applause.

2. I became _____ when the people seated behind me in the movie house continued talking once the film started.

3. I walked to the auditorium with a(n) _____ step as I looked forward to receiving an award.

4. The prisoner expected an early release for his _____ behavior.

5. Once the state had bought the waterfront land, it became a(n) _____ park.

> Read to find out why summer vacation was no longer boring for Ramona.

Questions:

1. Why was Beezus angry at her sister Ramona?

2. How did Ramona like to scare herself?

3. What was the purpose behind Mrs. Quimby's mysterious errands?

Chapter 2 (cont.)

4. What was the plan for sharing the new bedroom?

5. Why did Ramona think the summer was no longer boring?

Questions for Discussion:

1. Do you think Beezus and Ramona fight too much, or does their behavior seem normal?

2. Do you think Mrs. Quimby's plan for the girls to take turns living in the new bedroom was a good idea?

Art Connection:

Pretend you are getting a new bedroom that will be all your own. Draw a picture or a floor plan of what you would like in your bedroom. Write a label for each object.

Writing Activity:

Write about a time when you argued with another member of your family. Tell how this argument and future arguments might be avoided.

CHAPTER 3: THE HOLE IN THE HOUSE

Vocabulary: Use the context to help you select the best meaning for each underlined word in the following sentences. Circle the letter of the answer you choose.

1. Ramona was sure to <u>astound</u> the children in her class when she told them about the hole the builders chopped in her house.

   a. confuse   b. bore   c. amaze   d. annoy

2. Before the builders could add the room, they had to dig a trench for the <u>foundation</u>.

   a. color   b. window   c. roof   d. base

3. After standing near the building site all day, Ramona's hair looked <u>dingy</u> from the dust.

   a. dull   b. bright   c. rusty   d. shaggy

Word Study: Prefixes and Word Roots

Read the following sentence:

> Ramona felt <u>impatient</u> when she found out about her new room.

The root word is "patience." The prefix is "im."

The prefix "im" means <u>not</u>. The word "impatient" means <u>not patient</u>. What do each of the following words mean?

1. imperfect   _____

2. impossible   _____

3. impolite   _____

4. impure   _____

> Read to find out whether Ramona had fun while the new room was being built.

Chapter 3 (cont.)

Questions:

1. Why was Ramona excited about the new room?
2. Why did Ramona and Howie enjoy the game of brick factory?
3. Why did Mrs. Quimby put up with the game?
4. What event made the children end their daily game of brick factory?
5. How did Ramona and Beezus feel about the hole in the house?

Questions for Discussion:

1. Do you think you would be allowed to play brick factory at your home?
2. Have you or anyone you know lived through a construction project at home? Was it a good or a bad experience?

Art Connection:

Ramona put her own personalized initial into the new, wet cement. It was a "Q" turned into a cat. Create personalized initials for your own name using the first letters of your first name and last name.

Writing Activity:

Once the hole was made in the house, Beezus and Ramona entertained themselves at bedtime by making up spooky stories about the hole. Write an original spooky story telling about what might come in through the hole in the house. You and your classmates may share your stories.

CHAPTER 4

Vocabulary: Antonyms are words with opposite meanings. Draw a line from each word in column A to its antonym in column B. Then use the words in column A to fill in the blanks in the sentences below.

A	B
1. eager	a. permanent
2. modest	b. embarrassed
3. temporary	c. increase
4. dwindle	d. reluctant
5. proud	e. boastful

. . . .

1. Ramona enjoyed the hole in the house, knowing it was a(n) _____ situation.

2. Mrs. Quimby was _____ of herself for getting a part-time job.

3. The entire Quimby family was _____ for the builders to complete the room.

4. Ramona wanted to appear _____ when she told about the new room that was being built on her house.

5. When the children all laughed at her, Ramona felt her confidence _____.

> Read to find out if first grade lives up to Ramona's expectations.

Questions:

1. How did Ramona feel about starting first grade?

2. What was the first thing that upset Ramona in class?

Chapter 4 (cont.)

3. How did Mrs. Griggs, the first grade teacher, compare with Miss Binny, Ramona's kindergarten teacher?

4. How did the class react to Ramona's show-and-tell story? Why do you think they reacted this way?

Questions for Discussion:

1. How do you think Mrs. Griggs could have made Ramona's first day better?

2. How do you think Ramona could have made her first day better?

Writing Activity:

Remember your first day in the first grade. Write about that day, recalling your teacher, the children you met, and the things that you did. Also, tell about your feelings. Were you scared? Did you look forward to the second day of school? If you have trouble remembering, ask others in your family for help.

CHAPTER 5

Vocabulary: Use the words inside the owl to fill in the blanks in the paragraph below.

spectacles
tattletale
owl
destroys
coping

The teacher put on her _____ [1] and began reading from her assignment book. "This week," she said, "everyone must do a research report on the _____. [2] There must be no _____ [3] right from the book. Write your report on the computer. Then, if your little brother or sister or dog _____ [4] your work, do not be a(n) _____. [5] Just print another copy.

Read to find out if Ramona was a tattletale.

Questions:

1. Why did Ramona now think that kindergarten was better than first grade?
2. Why did Ramona destroy Susan's owl?
3. Why did Ramona feel guilty when her mother said, "Oh, poor baby"?
4. What was Ramona thinking when she confided that "She wanted the girl in the mirror to like her"?

Chapter 5 (cont.)

Questions for Discussion:

1. Do you think Ramona should have torn up Susan's owl? In what other ways might she have handled the problem?

2. Which do you think was better—kindergarten or first grade?

Classification Activity: Good News/Bad News

In this chapter Ramona gets good news and bad news. Below are some things that happen. Put each phrase under the right heading.

- no time for show-and-tell
- answered math problem correctly
- Susan copied her owl
- tore up Susan's owl
- new room is finished
- great idea for wise owl

Good News	Bad News

Chapter 5 (cont.)

Literary Device: Simile

A simile is a comparison between two unlike objects using the words "like" or "as." What is being compared in this simile?

The sun hung in the sky like an orange volleyball.

_____ is being compared to _____

Make up your own similes by completing the sentences below.

1. Butterflies flew like_____

   _____.

2. Ramona's eyes were tear-stained and puffy like_____

   _____.

3. She ran as fast as _____

   _____.

4. The owl was as handsome as _____

   _____.

Writing Activities:

1. Imagine that you are Ramona's mother and your daughter has just torn up Susan's paper bag owl. Write a short letter of apology or explanation to Susan's mother.

2. Write about a time when you or someone you know felt guilty for an action that was done. Describe the action and tell whether you now think it was right to feel guilty.

CHAPTER 6

Vocabulary: Use the context to help you figure out the meaning of the underlined word in each of the following sentences. Then compare your definition with a dictionary definition.

1. Ramona drew a deep breath, enjoying the <u>fragrance</u> of new wood.

   Your definition _____

   Dictionary definition_____

2. When Ramona's imaginary elevator made its imaginary <u>descent</u> from the second floor, she stepped out into the real first floor.

   Your definition _____

   Dictionary definition_____

3. Beezus and Ramona were warned not to <u>reveal</u> the family secrets.

   Your definition _____

   Dictionary definition_____

4. When Mrs. Griggs smiled her <u>unyielding</u> smile, Ramona knew there was no way out of her difficult assignment.

   Your definition _____

   Dictionary definition_____

   > Read to find out why Ramona spent a whole night worrying.

Questions:

1. Why was Ramona worried about Parents' Night?
2. Why did Ramona have trouble falling asleep during the first night in her new room?
3. What showed that Ramona was really a clever little girl?
4. Why did Ramona leave a note for her mother?
5. How did Ramona make her public apology worthless?

Chapter 6 (cont.)

Questions for Discussion:

1. Do you think Mrs. Kemp was a good sitter?
2. Which do you think is the worst punishment—being scolded, being docked, or having someone you love express disappointment in you?
3. Do you think Ramona should be made to apologize to Susan?
4. Why do you think Ramona preferred a teacher who got excited to one who was always calm?
5. Do you think Ramona will tell her parents what happened when she apologized?

Literary Device: Simile

What is being compared in the following passage?

Ramona lay in bed with her thoughts as jumbled as a bag of jacks.

_____

What does this tell you about Ramona?

_____

_____

Math Connection:

Here is a subtraction problem that is more interesting than Mrs. Griggs's problem. Draw a picture to help you find the solution.

	Work Space
Beezus bought a pizza to share with Ramona and 3 other friends. If the pizza had 8 slices, how many could have a second slice?	

Answer: _____.

Writing Activity:

Imagine you are Ramona and you decide to warn your parents about what they may learn on Parents' Night. Write a letter to them describing the owl incident. Try to justify your actions to them.

CHAPTER 7

Vocabulary: Cross out the word that does not belong in each of the following word groups. Then tell how the other words are alike on the line below.

1. sandals   oxfords   mittens   boots

   These words are alike because _____

   _____.

2. loiter   rush   dawdle   idle

   These words are alike because _____

   _____.

3. bathrobe   pillow   blanket   sheet

   These words are alike because _____

   _____.

4. rose   clover   tulip   zinnia

   These words are alike because _____

   _____.

5. blink   taste   squint   stare

   These words are alike because _____

   _____.

6. curtain   blind   carpet   shade

   These words are alike because _____

   _____.

> Read to find out why Ramona is afraid of going to bed at night.

Chapter 7 (cont.)

Questions:

1. Why did Ramona think her days were bad?

2. Why did Ramona stall before going to bed?

3. Why wouldn't Ramona ask to return to her old room?

4. What did Mr. Cardoza have to do with changing Ramona's mood?

Questions for Discussion:

1. Have you ever stalled at bedtime? What are some of the things you do?

2. Do you think Mrs. Quimby should have understood why Ramona was stalling at bedtime? How might she have helped Ramona?

3. How do you think Mr. Cardoza knew Ramona?

Literary Device: Metaphor

A metaphor is a suggested comparison between two unlike objects that does not use the words "like" or "as." For example:

> She [Ramona] closed her new curtains, shutting out the dark eye of the night.

What is being compared?

_____

What does this show about Ramona's feelings?

_____

_____

Chapter 7 (cont.)

Writing Activity: In this chapter Ramona had a bad dream. Tell about a dream that frightened you, or make up a scary dream.

One night I had a very scary dream. In this dream _____

_____

_____.

I tried to _____

but I could not _____

_____.

Then, much to my surprise, _____

_____.

Finally, _____

_____.

When I awoke, _____

_____.

CHAPTER 8

Vocabulary: Draw a line from each word on the left to its meaning on the right. Then use the numbered words to fill in the blanks in the sentences below.

1. solitude   a. upright; honest

2. conscientious   b. overstating; magnifying beyond truth

3. exaggerating   c. rebellious; insolent

4. defiant   d. extremely tired

5. exhausted   e. flabby; lacking stiffness

6. limp   f. state of being alone

. . . .

1. The team was _____ after running for miles in the hot sun.

2. If you are a(n) _____ student, you will do your homework every night.

3. After being in noisy crowds all day, I enjoyed the _____ of my own room.

4. I know my sister is _____ when she says that she is the smartest person in the entire school.

5. The flag became _____ when it was left out in the rain by mistake.

6. The little boy became _____ when he was accused of mischief that he didn't do.

> Read to find out why Ramona screamed a bad word.

Chapter 8 (cont.)

Questions:

1. Why did Ramona hide her progress report?

2. What did Ramona do to show her anger for her teacher and school? How did her family react to this?

3. How do you know that the family really sympathized with Ramona?

4. What did Mrs. Quimby mean when she said that "love isn't like a cup of sugar"?

5. Why wouldn't Mr. Quimby try to change Ramona's class?

Questions for Discussion:

1. Were you surprised about the way Ramona's parents reacted to their daughter's progress report?

2. Do you think Mrs. Griggs was fair in her report about Ramona?

3. What do you think Ramona might do to make the rest of her school year better?

Writing Activity:

Write about a time when you or someone you know tried to hide some information from your family. Describe the information and tell why it was hidden. Finally, indicate whether the information was ever revealed, and if so, what was the outcome?

CHAPTER 9

Vocabulary: Use the context to figure out the meaning of the underlined word in each of the following sentences. Then answer the question below each sentence.

1. My neighbor was so worried about his lawn, that he put up a sign warning people not to <u>trespass</u>.

    When you <u>trespass</u> on someone's property, do you

    a. plant flowers in the garden?

    b. go where you don't belong?

    c. build a house?

2. You might consider yourself in <u>peril</u> if you come upon a large, growling dog.

    Ramona felt she was in <u>peril</u> when she saw a police dog. Do you think the dog is

    a. dangerous?

    b. friendly?

    c. tired?

3. You might go to a parent or a teacher for help if you have a <u>predicament</u>.

    Are you in a <u>predicament</u> when

    a. you forget your part in a play?

    b. you bring in something to show for show-and-tell?

    c. you do your homework perfectly?

4. We watched the dog take his bone to the far corner of the room, lie down, and <u>gnaw</u> on his bone.

    When you <u>gnaw</u> on something do you

    a. tear it apart viciously?

    b. nibble on it?

    c. swallow it whole?

Chapter 9 (cont.)

5. If you have poor eyesight, you should be extremely <u>cautious</u> when crossing the street.

    If you are <u>cautious</u> would you

    a. look both ways before you cross the street?

    b. talk to strangers?

    c. go skydiving?

> Read to find out how Ramona proves she is her father's spunky daughter.

Questions:

1. Why did Ramona feel spunky as she walked to school?

2. How did Ramona lose one shoe?

3. Why did Ramona begin to like Mrs. Griggs?

4. Why did Ramona walk into Mr. Cardoza's room?

5. Why did Ramona finally feel she was brave?

Questions for Discussion:

1. Do you think Ramona's attitude had caused some or all of her first-grade problems?

2. In what ways did Ramona grow up during her year in first grade?

3. What do you think might have happened if Ramona had changed classes?

4. Would you want to have someone like Ramona as a friend? Why?

Literary Device: Irony

Irony refers to a twist of fate in which something unexpected happens. What is ironic about Mrs. Griggs finally choosing Ramona to lead the flag salute?

_____

_____

Writing Activity:

Write about the ways you have grown up since the beginning of the school year. Describe what you were like then and tell how you have changed.

CLOZE ACTIVITY

The following passage has been taken from Chapter Seven. Read it through completely, and then go back and fill in each blank with a word that makes sense.

   The moment Ramona dreaded had come. There was no one awake to _____ [1] her. Ramona tried to lie as _____ [2] and as still as a paper _____ [3] so that Something slithering under the _____ [4] and slinking around the walls would _____ [5] know she was there. She kept _____ [6] eyes wide open. She longed for _____ [7] father to come home; she was _____ [8] to stay awake until morning.

   Ramona _____ [9] of Beezus safely asleep in the _____ [10] dark of the room they had _____ [11] shared. She thought of the way _____ [12] used to whisper and giggle and _____ [13] scare themselves. Even their quarrels were _____ [14] than being alone in the dark. _____ [15] ached to move, to ease her _____ [16] rigid from lying still so long, _____ [17] she dared not. She thought of _____ [18] black gorilla with fierce little eyes _____ [19] the book in her bookcase and _____ [20] to shove the thought out of _____ [21] mind. She listened for cars on the _____ [22] street and strained her ears for _____ [23] sound of a familiar motor. After _____ [24] seemed like hours and hours, Ramona _____ [25] the sound of the Quimby car _____ [26] into the driveway. She went limp _____ [27] relief. She heard her father unlock _____ [28] back door and enter. She heard _____ [29] pause by the thermostat to turn _____ [30] the furnace. She heard him turn off the living-room light and tiptoe down the hall.

POST-READING ACTIVITIES

1. Why do you think this book is called *Ramona the Brave*?

    _____

    Write another title for the book that would also be good.

    _____

2. Do you think that Ramona's parents are fair when their daughter has
    a problem? Explain.

    How would your parents feel if:
    *   you lost a shoe on the way to school?
    *   you were afraid to sleep alone in a new room?
    *   you told them your teacher didn't like your work?
    *   you tattled on a classmate?

3. Make a time line for the book. Write four important events along this
    line in the order in which they happened. The first one is done for you.

1	2	3	4
Ramona learns she will have her own room.			

4. Ramona always used her vivid imagination to explain how extraordi-
    nary things happened. Imagine you are Ramona explaining how the
    dog chewed up your shoe.

    One my way to school this morning I met_____

    _____ .

    This is what happened to me. _____

    _____

    _____

    _____

    _____

BOOK REVIEW

The book *Ramona the Brave* by Beverly Cleary is about some of the problems Ramona had when she entered first grade. Complete the book review below.

The first day, during show-and-tell, Ramona tries to tell about

_____. The children

laugh because _____

_____. Her teacher is annoyed and thinks

she is _____.

Another time when Ramona feels her teacher doesn't like her is

_____

_____.

Ramona is helped by _____ who tells her to

be spunky. She shows her courage when _____

_____

_____.

My favorite part of the book is _____

_____

_____.

I did/did not like the book because _____

_____

_____.

I think that _____

would like to read this book because _____

_____

_____.

SUGGESTIONS FOR FURTHER READING

* Atwater, Richard. *Mr. Popper's Penguins*. Random House.

Cone, Molly. *Mishmash*. Simon & Schuster.

_____. *Mishmash and the Sauerkraut Mystery*. Simon & Schuster.

_____. *Mishmash and the Substitute Teacher*. Simon & Schuster.

Conford, Ellen. *Dreams of Victory*. Scholastic.

* Danziger, Paula. *Amber Brown is Not a Crayon*. Scholastic.

* _____. *Amber Brown Goes Fourth*. Scholastic.

Kandell, Lenny. *Smart Aleck*. Simon & Schuster.

_____. *The Revenge of the Incredible Dr. Rancid and His Youthful Assistant Jeffrey*. Scholastic.

Hurwitz, Johanna. *What Goes Up Must Come Down*. Scholastic.

* MacLachlan, Patricia. *Seven Kisses in a Row*. HarperCollins.

* Manes, Stephen. *Be a Perfect person in Just Three Days*. Random House.

* Park, Barbara. *Junie B. Jones and the Stupid, Smelly Bus*. Random House.

* _____. *Junie B., First Grader (at last!)*. Random House.

Sachs, Marilyn. *A Secret Friend*. Scholastic.

* Sharmat, Marjorie W. *Maggie Marmelstein for President*. HarperCollins.

* Taylor, Theodore. *The Trouble With Tuck*. HarperCollins.

* Warner, Gertrude. *The Boxcar Children*. Albert Whitman.

* Williams, Margery. *The Velveteen Rabbit*. HarperCollins.

Some Other Books by Beverly Cleary

Beezus and Ramona. HarperCollins.

* *Dear Mr. Henshaw*. HarperCollins.

Ellen Tebbits. HarperCollins.

* *The Mouse and the Motorcycle*. HarperCollins.

* *Muggie Maggie*. HarperCollins.

Ramona and Her Father. HarperCollins.

Ramona and Her Mother. HarperCollins.

* *Ramona Forever*. HarperCollins.

Ramona the Pest. HarperCollins.

* *Ramona Quimby Age 8*. HarperCollins.

* *Socks*. HarperCollins.

* *Strider*. HarperCollins.

* NOVEL-TIES Study Guides are available for these titles.

ANSWER KEY

Chapter 1

Vocabulary:
1. e 2. d 3. f 4. b 5. a 6. c; 1. exasperating 2. errands 3. subdued 4. reluctant 5. triumphant 6. confidence

Questions:
1. Ramona was eager to tell her mother what had happened in the park because this was the first time she had defended her big sister Beezus, and she was proud of herself. 2. Ramona felt proud because she had done something grown up and spoken up to big boys. 3. Mrs. Quimby told Beezus to ignore the boys if she were teased again. 4. Ramona was bored with summer vacation because she had nobody to play with. 5. Beezus got her nickname because Ramona had been unable to pronounce "Beatrice," her sister's real name, when she was little.

Sequence:
5, 3, 1, 4, 2, 6

Chapter 2

Vocabulary:
1. c 2. b 3. d 4. e 5. a; 1. enthusiasm 2. indignant 3. jaunty 4. virtuous 5. public

Questions:
1. Beezus was angry at Ramona because she had broken her red crayon. 2. Ramona scared herself by looking at a picture of a gorilla. 3. The purpose of Mrs. Quimby's errands was to get a part-time job and secure a bank loan for a new room they would build. 4. The plan was for each girl to have the new room for six months. 5. Ramona no longer thought the summer was boring because she was excited by the construction project and looked forward to having something to discuss for show-and-tell.

Chapter 3

Vocabulary:
1. c 2. d 3. a

Word Study:
1. not perfect 2. not possible 3. not polite 4. not pure

Questions:
1. Ramona was excited because she could have her own room and she could tell her class about it. 2. Ramona and Howie enjoyed the game of brick factory because it made them feel strong and powerful. 3. Mrs. Quimby allowed the children to play brick factory because it kept Ramona amused and outdoors. 4. The arrival of the construction workers ended the game of brick factory. They needed the driveway for their equipment. 5. Ramona and Beezus were both excited and scared by the hole in the house.

Chapter 4

Vocabulary:
1. d 2. e 3. a 4. c 5. b; 1. temporary 2. proud 3. eager 4. modest 5. dwindle

Questions:
1. Ramona felt excited, eager, and grown up about starting first grade. 2. Ramona was upset when her teacher called her Ramona Kitty Cat and the class meowed. 3. Miss Binney was young and sensitive to Ramona's feelings. Mrs. Griggs was older, more formal, and had less of a sense of humor. 4. The class laughed when Ramona gave her show-and-tell. They thought Ramona invented a ridiculous story.

Chapter 5

Vocabulary:
1. spectacles 2. owl 3. copying 4. destroys 5. tattletale

Questions:
1. Ramona remembered that in kindergarten they had fun drawing outside. First grade was boring. 2. Ramona destroyed Susan's owl because she was angry that Susan had copied her owl and then was praised for her work by the teacher. 3. Ramona felt she had been so bad she didn't deserve to be comforted. 4. Ramona wanted to get people's approval. She wanted to be more likable.

Classification:
Good News—answers math problem correctly, new room is finished, great idea for wise owl. Bad News—no time for show-and-tell, Susan copied her owl, tore up Susan's owl.

Chapter 6

Vocabulary:
1. fragrance–pleasant smell 2. descent–movement downward 3. reveal–make known 4. unyielding–rigid; not inclined to give in

Questions:
1. Ramona was worried about Parents' Night because she didn't want her parents to find out that she destroyed Susan's owl. 2. Ramona was afraid to sleep alone in her new room and she was feeling guilty. 3. Ramona showed that she was intelligent when she was able to write a note to her parents and she could read some of the newspaper. 4. Ramona left a note for her mother so that she could learn what Mrs. Griggs told her on back-to-school night. 5. Ramona made her public apology worthless when she muttered to Susan as she returned to her desk, "Even if you are a copycat who—*stinks!*"

Math Connection:
3 people could have a second slice.

Chapter 7

Vocabulary:
1. mittens—The other words all name a type of footwear. 2. rush—The other words all name a slow, nondirected action. 3. bathrobe—The other words all name items that appear on a bed. 4. clover—The other words all name a kind of flower. 5. taste—The other words all name something done with the eyes. 6. carpet—The other words all name a window covering.

Questions:
1. Ramona thought her days were bad because she felt her teacher didn't like her. 2. Ramona stalled before going to bed because she was scared of sleeping alone in her new room. 3. Ramona thought that she would be admitting defeat and acting like a baby if she asked to return to her old room. 4. Ramona became happy when an upper-grade teacher knew her identity.

Chapter 8

Vocabulary:
1. f 2. a 3. b 4. c 5. d 6. e; 1. exhausted 2. conscientious 3. solitude 4. exaggerating 5. limp 6. defiant

Questions:
1. Ramona hid her progress report because she was afraid that it said terrible things about her. 2. Ramona expressed her anger by shouting what she thought was a bad word—GUTS. The family was amused. 3. It was clear that Ramona's family sympathized with her when Mr. and Mrs. Quimby did not appear angry and Beezus told about times when she had been misunderstood. 4. Mrs. Quimby meant that there was enough love for both of her daughters. 5. Mr. Quimby wouldn't agree to change Ramona's class because he thought his daughter should be able to adjust to many different personalities.

Chapter 9

Vocabulary: 1. b 2. a 3. a 4. b 5. a

Questions:
1. Ramona felt spunky because her father had given her confidence to try to turn over a new leaf. 2. Ramona threw her shoe at a dog that was threatening her. The dog chewed on the shoe and forgot about Ramona. 3. Ramona began to like Mrs. Griggs when she showed sympathy for her shoe problem. 4. Ramona went to Mr. Cardoza's room because she needed a stapler to make herself a paper-towel slipper. She hoped that Mr. Cardoza would treat her in a grown-up fashion as he had before. 5. Ramona felt brave when the school secretary looked at Ramona's shoe and said how brave Ramona must have been.